D0435123

EPIC FAILS

THE WRIGHT BROTHERS:
NOSE-DIVING INTO HISTORY

EPIC FAILS

THE WRIGHT BROTHERS: NOSE-DIVING INTO HISTORY

ERIK SLADER AND BEN THOMPSON

ILLUSTRATIONS BY **TIM FOLEY**

Roaring Brook Press

New York

For our families

Library of Congress Control Number: 2017957500
Hardcover ISBN: 978-1-250-15055-4
Paperback ISBN: 978-1-250-15056-1

Our books may be purchased in bulk for promotional, educational, or
business use. Please contact your local bookseller or the Macmillan
Corporate and Premium Sales Department at (800) 221-7945 ext. 5442
or by e-mail at MacmillanSpecialMarkets@macmillan.com.

First edition, 2018
Book design by Monique Sterling
Printed in the United States of America by LSC Communications,
Harrisonburg, Virginia

Hardcover: 10 9 8 7 6 5 4 3 2 1
Paperback: 10 9 8 7 6 5 4 3 2 1

"Never interrupt someone doing something you said couldn't be done."

—Amelia Earhart

CONTENTS

Failure at Kitty Hawk

July, 1901

If at first you don't succeed . . . you're not the only one. In fact, you're in pretty good company.

On a hot summer day in 1901, Wilbur and Orville Wright stood atop a sand dune in the small town of Kitty Hawk, North Carolina. After a few promising tests with their first glider the previous year, Wilbur and Orville had saved up money for a new aircraft. They worked on it day and night, thought about it nonstop, and finally constructed an improved glider, a biplane that weighed ninety-eight pounds and had a wingspan of twenty-two feet. After months of calculations, blueprints, and hard work, they'd constructed a machine that they believed would actually take a human up into the air and keep him there. This was the thing that would succeed where humans had failed for centuries.

Despite numerous setbacks, unbearably hot weather, and a relentless onslaught of mosquitoes, the brothers stood strong and stayed optimistic about their latest test. They had even invited a crowd of locals to gather on the scorching sand dunes of Kill Devil Hills to witness what would surely be a historic moment.

Wilbur climbed aboard and stretched himself out horizontally on the wing. With Orville's help, the craft lurched forward over the edge of the hill and into the wind. For a brief moment, Wilbur soared through the air. Seconds later he fell through the air, spiraling into an ungraceful and terrifying nosedive. As the bystanders watched, Wilbur Wright and his wooden glider face-planted into a sandy dune.

Undeterred except for a slightly bruised ego

(people laughing at you is never all that much fun), Wilbur got back up, dusted himself off, and got ready for another try. His next attempts at flight were even less successful. Once the wind even blew the glider backward.

Several more failed attempts later, Wilbur barely managed to limp away from the busted biplane. The wooden airframe was smashed, Wilbur was bruised and bloody, and the crowd of spectators had left hours before.

There was no denying it: No history would be made that day. The Wright brothers' "new and improved" glider was a failure. A miserable pile of wreckage strewn across the sand. As the two dragged their battered glider back to their camp, Wilbur turned to his brother and said, "Man will not fly for fifty years."

This was their crossroads. Their moment of truth. They could have given up, gone back to their bike shop, and disappeared into time forever.

Instead, they decided not to let this failure stop them from achieving their dreams. Before they even returned home to Ohio, Orville and Wilbur Wright vowed to push on, draw up new plans, and not give up until they'd accomplished their goals.

Wilbur had said that man wouldn't fly for fifty years. But it took him and Orville only two more to prove that statement wrong.

CHAPTER 1
Learning to Fall

"There is an art to flying . . . The knack lies in learning how to throw yourself at the ground and miss."
—Douglas Adams (*Life, the Universe and Everything*)

Since the dawn of time, mankind has looked to the skies and dreamed of doing the impossible: soaring effortlessly through the air with the grace of a bird, banking and gliding hundreds of feet above the Earth. It's a dream humans have clung to since the beginning of written language, dating back to the ancient Greek myth of Icarus, a tale about a boy who was able to escape

the tower of an evil king by flying out his prison window on a pair of birdlike wings his father built for him out of feathers and wax.

Of course, Icarus was also the earliest recorded Epic Fail of human flight. Because he was having so much fun flying around like a maniac, Icarus climbed too high in the sky, and the sun melted the wax holding his feathered wings together. The wings disintegrated, and Icarus plummeted hundreds of feet to his untimely death. People today still use the expression "don't fly too close to the sun" when they try to warn you not to do something stupid.

Despite the cautionary tale of Icarus, people

still tried to figure out how to make a man fly. As you might have noticed, this isn't a particularly easy thing to do. Humans aren't really designed to fly through the air like beakless pterodactyls. We don't have wings, we don't have jetpacks embedded in our feet, we aren't particularly graceful animals, and we don't draw power from Earth's yellow sun as Superman does when he flies. So where do you start?

In 852 CE a daredevil inventor named Armen Firman tried to get it done straight up Icarus-style. He put on a huge cloak with wooden struts holding it open (it kind of looked like a wingsuit), wallpapered it in feathers, and jumped off the tallest tower in Córdoba, Spain.

Much to his surprise, but to no one else's, he plummeted to the ground almost immediately. As he was falling, however, something interesting happened—his homemade glider caught the wind for a moment, and it actually slowed his fall a little. It didn't slow Armen down enough that he didn't break nearly every bone in his body, but sometimes making discoveries can be quite painful.

This wacky stunt inspired a scholar named Abbas Ibn Firnas to spend his life pursuing what it would really take to glide in the wind. Abbas was a Muslim mathematician, engineer, chemist, and inventor who had designed everything from water clocks to astronomical star charts. Abbas may have witnessed Armen Firman's flight (in fact, the history here is so sketchy that he and Firman *might have even been the same guy*) and decided to spend the next several decades studying the flight of birds, their wingspans, and their graceful movements through the air.

At the age of sixty-five, a full twenty-three years after Armen Firman's "flight," Abbas Ibn Firnas constructed a glider of silk, wood, and vulture feathers; ignored the naysayers who told him he was just going to splat himself like a water balloon; and made his way to the tallest cliff he could find. Fueled by determination, and with a large crowd from Córdoba watching from a nearby cliff, Abbas Ibn Firnas got a running start and took a flying leap of faith.

To the shock and surprise of the onlookers, Abbas Ibn Firnas did not immediately fall screaming to a painful death below. Instead, he glided through the air, soaring like a bird for an impressive amount of time. But Abbas's elation soon gave way to a pressing concern . . . because despite all the work he'd put into figuring out taking off and gliding through the air, he hadn't put much thought into how to actually maneuver the glider—or, perhaps more important, how to land it. Without any control over his descent, the poor guy came crashing to the ground like an oversize paper airplane.

Ibn Firnas did survive his unfortunate crash, but he hurt his back so badly he would walk with a limp for the rest of his life and never tried to fly again. Nowadays, there's a crater on the moon named after him, in honor of his achievement—although possibly in homage to the crater he left when he smacked into the ground like Wile E. Coyote.

Over the centuries that followed, others kept the dream of flight alive, but with little success. An English monk named Roger Bacon hypothesized the possibility of a "flying engine" in 1260, but he never actually built one. In the 1300s Italian explorer Marco Polo wrote of Chinese kites that could hoist a man into the air, although he didn't bring one of those kites back to Europe and was known for making up more than a few details about his trips, so who knows. In 1507 Italian John Damian covered himself in chicken feathers and tried to fly off Stirling Castle in Scotland, but no matter how hard he flapped his arms, he just rocketed toward the ground like a big flesh-colored rock. It wasn't a soft landing for poor Mr. Damian.

It would seem that before man would learn to fly, he'd have to learn how to fall. And probably also how to land.

A FLIGHT OF FAILURE

Besnier the Locksmith

Besnier was a French locksmith who became obsessed with human flight, so in 1678 he developed a harness to achieve just that. Besnier's flying apparatus looked absolutely ridiculous— it used two wooden paddles strapped to each of his limbs as part of a "flapping mechanism."

More Failed Attempts at Powered Human Flight

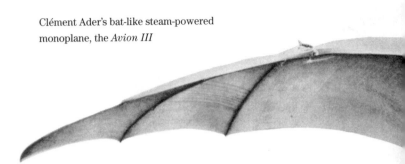

Clément Ader's bat-like steam-powered monoplane, the *Avion III*

The crazy thing is—it worked! Well, sort of. He managed to glide short distances surprisingly well, but longer distances proved challenging and dangerous.

Pierre Desforges

An eccentric French clergyman, Pierre Desforges, was convinced humans could fly like birds if only they had wings. In 1770 he constructed a pair of wings, but instead of trying them out himself, he tried to get peasants to volunteer for him. Later on he attached a twenty-foot wingspan to a six-foot gondola and tried to

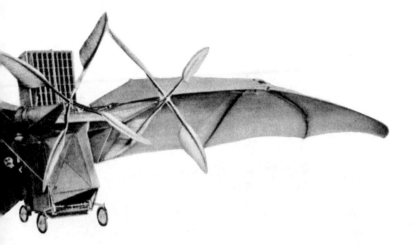

soar off one of his church's lookout towers—
he didn't. Instead, his gondola crashed to the
ground. Miraculously, he had only a broken arm
to show for it.

Clément Ader

Clément Ader was a French inventor who in-
vested almost all his time and money in developing experimental flying machines with little or
no success. His most promising attempt, though,
was a wooden and linen, bat-like steam-powered
monoplane called the *Avion III*. The 880-pound
aircraft had a fifty-two-foot wingspan. In 1897

the military gave the "aircraft" a test run. Unfortunately, the most it could do was hop a few inches off the ground. The military immediately cut funding.

Gustave Whitehead

Gustave Whitehead was a German aviation enthusiast who claimed to have flown his *No. 21* monoplane in 1901, before the Wright brothers,

Gianni Caproni's monstrous *Capronissimo Ca.60*, a nine-winged, eight-engined, 30-foot-high flying boat (that didn't fly)

but all evidence points to his design being aerodynamically unsound, and there was little evidence to back up his claim.

Gianni Caproni

In 1921 aviation pioneer Gianni Caproni tried to create a flying boat. The *Capronissimo Ca.60* was a nine-wing (!), eight-engine, thirty-foot-high, seventy-seven-foot-long boat with a wingspan of ninety-eight feet. It weighed 30,865 pounds! During its second test flight, soon after takeoff, the ridiculously expensive aircraft crashed into the water and completely broke apart. Caproni later commented, "The path of progress is strewn with suffering."

CHAPTER 2

The Problem with Gravity

1665–1783

"Once you have tasted flight, you will forever walk the earth with your eyes turned skyward, for there you have been, and there you will always long to return."
—Leonardo da Vinci

In 1665 an English mathematician named Isaac Newton was sitting under an apple tree when all of a sudden an apple fell and bonked him on the head. While the first words out of his mouth were probably not the kind of words we can print in a book like this, taking an apple to the dome also gave Isaac Newton a *eureka* moment.

At least, that's the story. In fact, the apple episode probably never happened. But still, Newton was a supergenius scientist and a determined experimenter who changed the way people

looked at the way the world works. Building off the research of famous scientists and astronomers such as Galileo Galilei and Johannes Kepler, Newton realized that everything in the cosmos is governed by the laws of physics and that gravity is one of the things that binds the universe together.

Without getting too much into it, the mass and rotation of the Earth generates an invisible force called *gravity*, which pulls everything toward the ground. It's the reason stuff falls when you drop it, and it's the reason you and I don't fly off into space. It's also, unfortunately, one of the reasons flight is so hard. Newton discovered that all objects, regardless of weight, fall at the same rate—that is, unless they catch the wind or are lighter than air.

He also realized that without an atmosphere, not even birds could fly. Using his laws of physics, the key to defying the power of gravity would be to use the air itself.

Easier said than done.

During the fifteenth and sixteenth centuries, an Italian artist and scientist got closer than ever before to achieving human aviation. Leonardo da Vinci painted the *Mona Lisa* and *The Last Supper*, but he wasn't just a famous painter. He was also a part-time inventor, architect, sculptor, cartographer, writer, historian, biologist, geologist, paleontologist, botanist, astrophysicist, and vegetarian. He wrote all his notes backward (in cursive!), invented the sniper rifle, and used to buy birds from pet stores so he could set them free outside.

Among his thousands of inventions and discoveries, Leonardo designed a number of "flying machines." In fact, more than thirty-five thousand words and five hundred sketches discovered from his notes were dedicated to the goal of human flight. He invented the concept of a parachute, designed a glider that looks like Batman's cape, and even drew schematics for a predecessor to the helicopter! Several practical and elaborate designs were thought up and sketched out by Leonardo at a time when most people still rode around on horses and fought one another with swords. Although some aeronautical engineers believe that Leonardo's human-powered flying machines may have actually worked, this multitasking genius unfortunately never had a chance to build or test any of his inventions.

It wasn't until 1783 that another leap forward was made. This time, it was two brothers, although not the ones you're probably thinking of. No, this was two Frenchmen named Joseph and Étienne Montgolfier, who created the world's first hot air balloon. Hot air is lighter than cool air, and the brothers came to realize that by harnessing it, they could create lift (this is the "lighter than air" idea we talked about when we discussed gravity earlier). On November 21, 1783, they made history in Paris when their gigantic, seven-story-tall balloon successfully

lifted the two men more than three thousand feet into the air!

Sailing through the air was pretty great, but once again that old problem of "How the heck do we land this thing?" meant that it wouldn't be a completely smooth ride. As the aeronauts drifted back toward the ground, the fire that heated the air in the balloon began to burn through the fabric, lighting the sides on fire! Together, the two men scrambled to put it out with wet sponges . . . which caused further problems, because putting out the fire meant that the balloon started to fall to the ground really, really fast. The brothers had to frantically relight the flames so the balloon would get a little more lift and not smack into the ground! After what must have been a pretty terrifying adventure, the Montgolfier brothers finally reached the ground safely . . . about five miles from where they were supposed to land.

The success of the Montgolfier brothers was further developed by Professor Jacques Charles, who used hydrogen instead of hot air in his balloon in 1783. Hydrogen is lighter than air, so it meant you could get better lift and wouldn't need such a huge balloon to get airborne.

It didn't take long before people started using balloons for important, practical, real-world purposes. Like fighting. In 1808 two French guys got into a fight over a lady and decided they'd solve their dispute with a duel. So they both went up in hot air balloons and started shooting at each other's balloons with their muskets.

Monsieur de Grandpré won when he put a hole in Monsieur Le Pique's balloon, sending Le Pique tumbling hundreds of feet to his death. A few years after this, in 1861, during the American Civil War, Union soldier Thaddeus Lowe became the first man to use a hot air balloon in battle. Lowe flew so high that he was able to see

the Confederate army, but while he was taking notes on troop positions, the balloon broke away from the rope holding it to the ground. Lowe drifted helplessly into enemy territory. When he landed, the Confederates captured him as a spy.

Throughout the late 1800s, balloons were still the only way for a person to fly. In 1873 famous French science-fiction author Jules Verne wrote a bestselling novel called *Around the World in Eighty Days*, which was about circling the globe in a hot air balloon, and in 1900 the awesomely named Count Ferdinand von Zeppelin, from Germany, created the first dirigible, a balloon with engines that was capable of being steered.

But still, despite all this success, drifting in a balloon just isn't the same thing as flying like a bird, and dirigibles are huge, slow, and hard to maneuver. So while Zeppelin was rocking out his new invention, two brothers in Kitty Hawk, North Carolina, took humanity's first steps toward developing a real-life airplane: a controlled, powered, heavier-than-air craft that could soar through the skies like a bird.

CHAPTER 3
Orville and Wilbur

1896

"The moment you doubt whether you can fly, you
cease for ever to be able to do it."

—J. M. Barrie (*Peter Pan*)

Wilbur and Orville Wright were brothers,
born four years apart, and they were best friends.
They were the sons of Milton Wright, a pastor for
the Church of the United Brethren in Christ in
Dayton, Ohio, and his wife, Susan. Milton was a
loving father who'd grown up on the frontier and
taught his children the value of self-reliance
and hard work, but he was also a lifelong reader

Wilbur and Orville Wright, circa 1876/1877

and kept an extensive library of literary classics, history books, and encyclopedias.

When Wilbur and Orville were kids, their father brought home a toy that sparked their imaginations: a small, primitive helicopter made from wood and rubber bands, based on a design by French aviation engineer Alphonse Pénaud. The brothers played with it until it broke, and then they built one out of stuff they found around the house and kept right on going. Even at an early age, they were hooked on the idea of building something that would fly.

Both boys were smart, capable, and determined, but they had very different personalities. Wilbur, the older brother, was soft-spoken, strait-laced, and generally stoic. He was remarkably intelligent, had a strong personal drive, and dressed in well-tailored suits. His younger brother, Orville, on the other hand, was more outgoing and fiery. Orville grew a big, bushy mustache, played the man-dolin, made homemade candy, and was often cheerfully optimistic and temperamental. In school, Orville was typically described as a class clown and a bit of a troublemaker. He

even got expelled once! You wouldn't think these two personalities would go together well, but Orville always listened to his older brother, and that helped keep things in line.

Wilbur did excellently in high school and was considering Yale for college, but his plans were dashed one fateful day when he was playing ice hockey and took a hockey stick to his face, smashing out most of his teeth, laying him out, and injuring him so badly he had to drop out of school to recover. Orville, worried about his brother, dropped out as well and never returned.

Despite never finishing high school, the brothers were well read, extremely practical, and inventive. They weren't going to let something like not having a diploma keep them from succeeding. After running a print shop together (Orville was a big-time newspaper fan), the boys decided in 1892 to get into the bicycle business. Cycling had recently become a national pastime, thanks to the invention of something called the "safety bicycle." Have you ever seen those old-timey bikes with the humongous front wheel and teeny-tiny back wheel? Those are called *penny-farthings*, and riding one isn't easy at all. Plus it's pretty easy to fall off them and hurt yourself (it's like falling off a regular bike, except you fall twice as far before you hit the asphalt). So in the 1880s someone invented the "safety bike" with two equal-size wheels, and pretty soon everyone forgot that penny-farthings even existed. The Wright brothers saw an opportunity to work on some-thing cool that they enjoyed, and to make some cash while doing it. So they opened a bike shop in Dayton, Ohio, just a few blocks from their home.

Business at the shop was going well for a couple of years until one day in 1896, when Orville fell ill from a brutal disease called typhoid fever. Nowa-days typhoid is treatable with antibiotics, but back then antibiotics hadn't been invented yet, and with Orville running a 105-degree fever, things looked really scary. Orville passed in and out of consciousness, usually waking up to either his brother, his dad, or his sister, Katharine, sitting at the foot of the bed watching over him.

While Wilbur hung around watching over his sleeping brother, he happened to pick up a copy of *McClure's Magazine* and read an article that would change the boys' lives forever. It was about an eccentric German genius named Otto

Otto Lilienthal's glider

Lilienthal, who had dedicated his life to the goal of achieving human flight. Lilienthal had been an engineer in the Prussian Army, owned a company that made steam engines, and in his spare time made sweeping advances in glider construction and the mechanics of aviation. He published his calculations, *Bird-flight as the Basis of Aviation*, in 1889, describing concepts for a fixed-wing flying machine that sounded a lot like a modern-day hang glider. Two years later

he put his theories to the test by building a glider out of muslin and wood and jumping off a huge hill he'd built in a park just outside Berlin.

Amazingly, it worked—Otto soared through the air. Sure, he didn't have a ton of control over it, but he kept improving his designs, and over the next five years he flew more than two thousand times with eighteen gliders. Thanks to the invention of photography, pictures of Otto's flights made their way across the world and inspired hundreds of men and women to follow in his footsteps—including Wilbur Wright as he sat in a dimly lit room in Dayton, Ohio, reading tales of Otto's exploits to his sick brother Orville.

THE WRIGHT
FAMILY

We've met Wilbur Wright (1867–1912) and Orville Wright (1871–1948), but they were just part of the Wright clan. Let's meet the rest of them:

Parents

Milton, *1828–1917.* Wilbur and Orville's father was a minister and later bishop in the Church of the United Brethren, and editor of the church's newspaper.

Susan, *1831–1889.* The daughter of a carriage builder, Wilbur and Orville's mother was skilled with all sorts of tools. She died from tuberculosis shortly before the brothers opened their bicycle shop.

Siblings

Reuchlin, *1861–1920.* Wilbur and Orville's oldest brother lived in Missouri and Kansas. Wilbur left him an inheritance in his will, but Reuchlin didn't want to accept it, saying he had never been a part of the brothers' airplane business.

Lorin, *1862–1939.* Lorin worked with Wilbur and Orville in their print shop, helped Katharine manage the bicycle shop while the brothers were away, and later worked for the Wright aircraft company.

Katharine, *1874–1929.* Katharine was the only one of the Wright children to attend college and worked as a teacher before becoming part of her brothers' airplane business.

CHAPTER 4
Destiny Calls

1899

*"If birds can glide for long periods
of time, then . . . why can't I?"*
—Orville Wright

For the men and women searching for the secrets of powered human flight, there was plenty of glory, excitement, and fame in pursuing their goal—but there was also an unspeakable, ridiculous amount of danger. Nothing was a better example of this than what happened in 1896, when the "Flying Man" Otto Lilienthal lost control of his glider, fell fifty feet, and broke his back on impact with the ground. He died the next day. His last words were "sacrifices must be made." He had no regrets, even in failure, not even in the face of his own death. For him, flight been worth it.

Orville Wright thought flight was worth the risk as well, and when he finally got back on his feet, the brothers decided to follow in Otto's foot-steps (hopefully with less dying, though). Right away they set about studying as much as they could. Since Google wasn't a thing in 1899, Wilbur contacted the Smithsonian Institution in Washington, DC, for any and all research available on aviation and human flight. They bought Otto's book. They also studied French inventor Octave Chanute's work in perfecting a glider's rigging system so it could safely carry a person. Before long, the Wright

brothers realized that becoming airborne wasn't the
problem—that had been done
tons of times, even dating back to
the dude who jumped off the tower in
Córdoba. The problem plaguing would-be
pilots in the 1890s was staying in the air, maneu-
vering the aircraft with any kind of efficiency,
and landing it without dying.

To help them on their quest, the Wrights started
observing birds in flight and taking note of how
they often swayed so effortlessly, changing direction with slight movements of their wings. One
day, while watching a flock of buzzards, Wilbur
had an epiphany.

He excitedly ran inside the house and dragged
Orville, Katharine, and one of her friends outside to show them an ordinary-looking cardboard box. Wilbur demonstrated the way in
which the box could warp when opposite ends

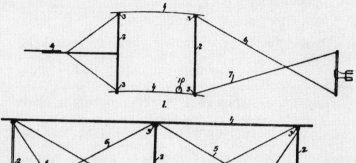

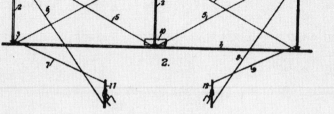

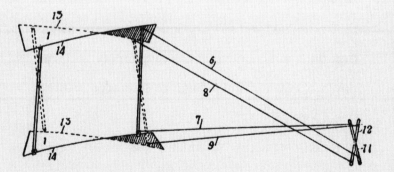

Wright brothers' drawings illustrating "wing-warping," a major secret to flight, which Wilbur discovered while playing with a cardboard box.

were pressed in, the same way a bird's wings twisted in flight to retain balance in the air. Wilbur explained that they could use the same basic rectangular structure for their aircraft design, with a mechanism to twist and warp the wings to balance it. Could this be the solution, or had Wilbur completely lost his mind?

During the summer of 1899, the two young men set to work on building their first aircraft in the loft above their bicycle shop on Dayton's West Third Street. It was a fifty-pound box-shaped glider, with two wings and a seventeen-foot wingspan, held together by a wooden frame and rigging system of crisscrossed ropes. All in all, the whole thing cost roughly fifteen dollars to construct, which doesn't sound like that much to you and me, but it shakes out to be $416 in today's money. Not a whole lot, but not exactly chump change, either.

The Wrights had tested a small prototype at

home and were confident enough to put their glider to a real-world test. Now all they needed was a good place to take off. Wilbur wrote a letter to Octave Chanute, asking for his opinion on good locations. Chanute happily responded and suggested either California or Florida for their windy coastlines, but if they were looking for a sandy beach with hills to launch from, they might have better luck farther up the East Coast.

The Wright brothers' search brought them into

contact with the United States Weather Bureau, which suggested Kitty Hawk, North Carolina. As it turned out, Kitty Hawk had everything they needed: wide-open spaces, strong and steady winds, and sandy dunes from which to launch their craft and land safely—plus relative privacy so there wouldn't be a lot of people around to point and laugh if Wilbur and Orville made complete fools of themselves.

Wilbur stole his sister's suitcase, bought a camera and tripod, packed a tent, and shipped out for North Carolina to get everything arranged. He took a train to Virginia and started asking people how to get to Kitty Hawk. Nobody had ever heard of the place. It was just a small, largely unpopulated speck on the North Carolina coast, and your average American in 1899 had no idea the town existed. Wilbur Wright was about to put it on the map.

Wilbur eventually ran into a boatman from

Kitty Hawk named Israel Perry, who offered to give him a ride down the river in a rickety little boat that didn't inspire a lot of confidence. Wilbur asked, "Is it safe?"

The answer he received didn't make Wilbur feel any better.

He later wrote about his terrifying boat ride. "The sails were rotten, the ropes badly worn and the rudder-post half rotted off, and the cabin so dirty and vermin-infested that I kept out of it from first to last." The run-down boat sprang a leak, and it fell to Wilbur to spend the entire forty-three-mile trip bailing river water with a bucket. Then, if that wasn't bad enough, a storm blackened the sky. Winds and rain tore the mainsail off the boat. Water flooded onto the deck. Yet still, Wilbur continued, pushing forward in search of a place few people had ever heard of so he could test a flying machine that was almost as likely to kill him as it was to make him a hero.

Wilbur Wright finally arrived at Kitty Hawk, a little shaken up but luckily still in one piece. He met up with a modest fisherman named William Tate and his wife, Addie, who gave Wilbur his first good meal in two days. Wilbur was extremely thankful for their hospitality, and when he explained his situation, the Tates told him they were more than happy to do whatever they could to help the Wright brothers on their quest.

Orville arrived in Kitty Hawk a few days after

Wilbur, although his route seems to have been less filled with danger and excitement. The brothers stayed with the Tate family, where they awkwardly shared what they described as "the most uncomfortable bed" they'd ever slept in. The next day, they got to work on assembling their glider for its first field test. It was time to make history . . . or die trying.

CHAPTER 5
The First Attempt

1900

"It is possible to fly without motors, but not without knowledge and skill."

—Wilbur Wright

It was a breezy autumn day in Kitty Hawk, North Carolina. Orville and Wilbur Wright stood on a sandy dune on the beach, each dressed like steampunk hipsters at Comic-Con in their goggles, tweed, and breeches. A lot of hard work and years of research had led them to this moment, and now it was time to put all their theories to the test.

The residents of Kitty Hawk knew about the two crazy Ohio boys who were trying to build a flying machine on the beach, and most of them were pretty skeptical. Many residents scoffed at the idea and dismissed the brothers as crackpots. None of this discouraged Orville and Wilbur. They didn't care what these people thought—flight was possible, and they were going to prove it.

When it was assembled, the Wright brothers' glider weighed fifty pounds and was sturdy enough to carry at least one passenger. The pilot would lie horizontally along the wing. In place of wheels, the "air craft" had wooden skis for landing gear, which seemed optimal considering it would land in sandy dunes and not on a flat asphalt runway.

The brothers set up camp on the Outer Banks, living off eggs, tomatoes, and any fish they managed to catch (which wasn't much). Orville

wrote to Katharine that he missed his corn bread and coffee, but especially his bacon. They had gone to Kitty Hawk because they needed the wind and sand for their invention to work, but the wind and sand were also reasons it wasn't a whole lot of fun to camp there. The brothers would usually wake up to the gritty spray of hot sand blowing right in their faces as they lay in their sleeping bags. Good times.

Tom Tate with dinner in front of the Wright's 1900 glider

Over the course of three days beginning on October 3, the Wright brothers ran tests on the craft for two to four hours at a time. "Learning the secret of flight from a bird was a good deal like learning the secret of magic from a magician," Orville wrote. They had yet to try flying with a pilot, instead focusing on observing the plane in the wind and testing its wing-warping apparatus by flying it almost like a kite. Everything was going fine until October 6, when an unexpected gust of wind picked up the glider and threw it like a football across the beach.

On October 3, 1900, the Wright brothers began testing their first aircraft, a fifty-pound glider, by flying it (unmanned) as a kite.

On October 6, the glider was all but destroyed in a storm.

Orville had been holding one of the ropes, and the gust yanked him clear off the ground. Not wanting to let go of his precious invention, he clung to the rope, trying to stop it even as the glider was chucked twenty feet through the air.

The plane crashed hard into the sand, smashing into bits. The Wrights could do nothing except take a picture of the wreckage before dragging it back to their tent in defeat. It was their first plane crash. It wouldn't be their last.

That night, the brothers considered throwing in the towel and calling it quits. Sitting by their campfire on the sand-whipped beach, they wondered if their dream of flight was to be over before it even got started.

No. Forget that. They hadn't gone all this way to give up, and the brothers resolutely decided to give it another shot. Renewed with a fresh sense of purpose, desire, and energy, Wilbur and Orville spent the next three days repairing their broken glider. At the same time, they started to attract attention from the locals. The residents were impressed by the boys' work ethic and helped direct them to the perfect location for their first attempt at manned flight: a place called Kill Devil Hills, just four miles from Kitty Hawk.

By October 19, the Wright brothers were ready for human trials. Wilbur and Orville, with the help of William Tate, dragged their newly repaired glider to the test site. There were no trees or bushes, but plenty of sand and three hills of varying heights, from thirty to one hundred feet. Most important, there was plenty of wind.

Wilbur Wright courageously climbed aboard the glider while everyone else cringed and crossed fingers. He got a tight grip on the controls. The wind picked up, catching the fabric of the flyer and pulling it toward the sky. Orville and William Tate let go of the reins holding the glider to the ground and watched as Wilbur was hoisted up into the air.

Holding on for dear life, Wilbur Wright soared

over the hills at an exhilarating speed. Thanks to the Wrights' innovative flight-control design, Wilbur was able to balance the craft as it approached the ground. He skidded to a bumpy stop at thirty miles an hour, which wasn't exactly fun, but it was still a much better landing than most of the aviators who came before him had achieved. After climbing out, Wilbur looked back and realized he'd just flown a distance of nearly four hundred feet—more than the distance of a football field! It hadn't been so much flying as it was falling with style, but for the Wrights it was just the encouragement they needed to keep going. They'd just made their first step toward success. They still had a long way to go, but this was a victory they felt incredibly proud to have accomplished.

Not long after they broke camp on October 23, a series of severe storms blew through and destroyed the Wright glider. In return for the Tates' help, the Wrights gave them what was left of their glider as a souvenir. William's wife, Addie, made dresses out of the fabric for their daughters.

CHAPTER 6
A Flight of Failure

1901

"I confess that in 1901 I said to my brother Orville

that man would not fly for fifty years."

—Wilbur Wright

After their first (mostly successful) test, the Wright brothers concluded that their glider could carry a person only in high winds and that it was too risky to try to maneuver it at any altitude. They had basically made a really big kite, not an airplane. The guys were determined to improve on the design and learn from their mistakes the next time around.

Even though they still ran their bike shop, the brothers spent nearly every waking hour for the next eight months contemplating any and all possible improvements to their glider. At one point, Wilbur and Orville argued so much that Katharine had to leave the house because they drove her crazy. They were so focused on their project that they had to hire a guy named Charlie Taylor to run their bicycle shop.

The Wrights' second glider was larger than their first design, sporting a twenty-two-foot wingspan. It also featured a protruding "nose," with a device called an "elevator" that was designed to help the pilot control the upward and downward angle of the plane midflight. By the time July 1901 came around, the Wrights were ready to head back to Kitty Hawk for round two.

This time, however, things did not go according to plan.

First, their trip was delayed by a hurricane. Then they were met with an uncomfortable heat wave that not only made everyone sweaty and cranky, but also didn't produce enough wind to

get enough lift for the glider. As if the weather wasn't enough, not long after building their base camp at Kill Devil Hills, the Wrights were greeted by swarming mosquitoes that actually ate through their socks and underwear! By the end of the week the brothers were covered head-to-toe in massive, itchy red welts and bites. Meanwhile, Katharine wrote to say that Charlie Taylor was a know-it-all and that she couldn't stand working with him.

If that wasn't bad enough, their second glider turned out to be a complete bust. Even worse, their hero, aviation pioneer Octave Chanute, was there to witness their embarrassment. Wilbur's first attempt failed spectacularly. Moments after takeoff, the craft spiraled into a nosedive. He tried again and again, repositioning himself each time with little success. On the final try, the glider took off, started flying *backward*, and then, when it crashed, ejected Wilbur from the wreckage. He smashed into the ground, limping away with a broken nose, a black eye, and a couple of bruised ribs. He'd gone to show off his designs to his boyhood idol and ended up humiliating himself. For all their "improvements," it seemed as though the Wrights had taken a step back. It quickly became apparent to them that this was the same problem that had cost Otto Lilienthal his life and that further testing would be dangerous until they managed to solve the problem with this glider's aerodynamics.

The Wrights stored their "new and improved" glider in the work shed they'd assembled, but both were destroyed during a series of windstorms. They salvaged what they could and returned to Ohio. Dejected, exhausted, and defeated, they barely spoke to each other on the long train ride home.

Did the Wrights consider calling it quits? You better believe it. They could have gone back to the bike shop and never built another glider for

Wilbur managed to stay aloft only briefly on the second glider before nose-diving into the sand dunes.

the rest of their lives. Is that what they did? Heck no.

They returned home, got an inspiring pep talk from Katharine, and immediately went back to the drawing board with more resolve than ever before. Unfortunately, they also faced some family drama. Their father, Milton Wright, was embroiled in a legal dispute with the church. Disagreements over policy led to his being stripped of his role as a bishop, which put considerable financial strain on the family.

Octave Chanute wrote to the Wrights, offering financial help from his good friend, multimillionaire entrepreneur Andrew Carnegie. The offer of cash did sound pretty good, but the Wright brothers were determined to pay their own way and were wary of becoming beholden to financial backers with ulterior motives. So they turned down a huge paycheck, got back to work on improving their bike models at the shop, and scrounged everything they could to fund their next aircraft.

Wilbur and Orville realized they couldn't rely on Otto's calculations for lift and drag—clearly, he didn't have that equation quite right. Instead, the brothers decided to run their own experiments. Using models and a small wind tunnel of their own design, they began to gather their own data.

By September 1902, after months of hard work, research, and saving up their hard-earned cash, they were ready to build a new and improved glider and face their demons again at Kill Devil Hills.

CHAPTER 7

If at First You Don't Succeed . . .

1902

"The airplane stays up because it doesn't have the time to fall."

—Orville Wright

The Wright brothers made a triumphant return to Kitty Hawk in September 1902, brimming with confidence in their new design and anxious to test it. They'd learned a lot from their trials and errors during the last trip, and their miserable defeat the year before had only inspired them to work twice as hard this time around.

After throwing out everything they'd learned from others, the Wrights believed they had finally cracked the code. Using data gathered from their experiments, they developed the lift equation—$L = kSV^2C_L$—and used it to calculate the proportions of their new aircraft, an eight-foot-tall biplane with a wingspan of thirty-two feet.

The residents of Kitty Hawk welcomed the

Wrights back, and the brothers were pretty happy that this time a throng of angry mosquitoes didn't immediately devour them upon arriving in town. Wilbur and Orville set up their base camp once again, and this time they rigged up their bikes so they could ride in the sand, an improvement that cut their trip between the town and the hills from three hours to one.

On September 19, 1902, they took the new glider out for a spin. It was a huge improvement over their last craft, but the controls were still difficult and sluggish, like trying to play a multiplayer computer game with a really bad Internet connection. The two brothers took turns gliding from Kill Devil Hills without incident for a couple of days, until suddenly something went wrong. Orville was flying when his controls stopped responding. Orville and the glider fell three stories before smashing hard into the sand. Miraculously, he was unharmed.

Two weeks later, on October 2, Orville couldn't sleep. As he tossed and turned in bed, the younger Wright brother suddenly had an epiphany: He theorized that the problem was that the rear rudder needed to be hinged rather than stationary, which would give the pilot more control. The next morning, during breakfast, he brought it up to his brother.

Wilbur and Orville, as close as they were, were also known for their sibling rivalry. They would often argue for hours over the smallest thing, each becoming more stubborn than the other. So when Orville suggested the change to the glider, he expected a fight. Instead, after a long sip of coffee, Wilbur nodded in agreement. When you're right, you're right. And (pardon the pun) Orville was right. The brothers set to work immediately.

Wilbur and Orville hadn't just perfected the biplane's structure, they had added a tail with a rudder—perhaps the most significant advance

October 10, 1902: Wilbur gliding. The aircraft's improved rudder is clearly visible.

in the history of aviation. The Wrights now had the world's first aircraft that could be controlled along all three axes:

- *Pitch*—The lateral tilt of an aircraft, the upward or downward direction of the plane's nose, controlled by the elevator. This controls lift and drag, helping the plane climb higher or dive down toward the ground. You know in the movies when they yell "Pull up!" and the guy pulls back on the control stick so the plane gains altitude and doesn't crash into a mountain? That's the plane rotating on the pitch axis.
- *Roll*—The rolling up or down on one side or the other, controlled by wing warping. This controls the equilibrium of the plane. You know the aircraft term "barrel roll," where the plane spins around in a circle? That's a good example of an aircraft rotating on the roll axis.
- *Yaw*—Movement of the plane from side to side in the direction of the flight, left or right, controlled

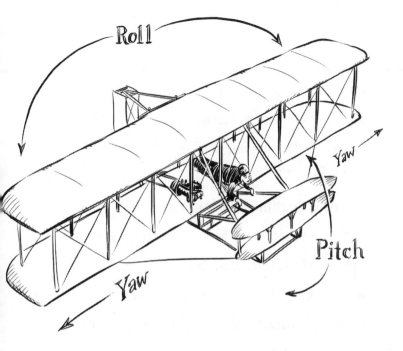

by the rudder. The rudder is typically used for minor adjustments, such as tweaking the approach to a runway. Bigger turns are usually executed using pitch and roll, like how a passenger airplane usually banks to the side after it takes off from the runway.

The difference in control was immediately noticeable, and the results would revolutionize the quest for flight. For the first time, they could circle, dive, soar, and land without any trouble at all. It worked. After all their hard work, they had solved the problem of controlling an aircraft in flight.

The only thing missing now was an engine.

During this time, Octave Chanute paid another visit to North Carolina, this time with his famous associate, another aviation pioneer named Augustus Herring. Chanute and Herring came to test their own glider: a triplane, which turned out to be a total bust. After witnessing the Wrights' unparalleled success, however, Chanute wrote to another colleague of his named Samuel Langley. Langley became very interested in the Wrights' progress and asked if he could come see this new plane of theirs.

Not wanting to reveal their secrets to a potential competitor, the Wright brothers said no.

CHAPTER 8

Fourth Time's a Charm

"The Wright brothers created the single greatest cultural force since the invention of writing."

—Bill Gates

In 1903 the Wright brothers unexpectedly found themselves in a race. Promising inventors around the world were working around the clock, and the Wrights were running out of time to earn the honor of *first in flight.*

Their biggest threat was the man they had told not to come visit them—Samuel Langley.

October 7, 1903: Langley's *Aerodrome* was catapulted from a houseboat—
and immediately fell into the Potomac River.

Langley was a brilliant inventor; he was close
to a breakthrough with his own team from
the Smithsonian Institute. On October 7, 1903,
pilot Charles Manly boarded Langley's steam-
powered *Aerodrome* to attempt a test flight
above the Potomac River. If it had worked, it
would have been the first successful powered
flight in human history. Instead, the $50,000,
fifty-two-horsepower plane surged forward and

immediately nose-dived into the water without ever leaving the ground.

The *San Francisco Call* reported: LANGLEY'S FLYING MACHINE FAILS COMPLETELY!

Meanwhile, the Wright brothers were hard at work perfecting their biplane. The only problem left to solve was how to generate lift and get off the ground without the help of wind. They would need an engine. But not just any motor would do; they needed something powerful enough to

lift the craft but light enough to not weigh it down too much.

Once again easier said than done.

The first internal combustion engine was created in 1886 by Karl Benz, a guy who today we probably know best as being the "Benz" in Mercedes-Benz. Up until this point, these clunky motors had been used to power only early automobiles, and no one had given much thought to making one as small and lightweight as possible.

Neither Wilbur nor Orville was much of a mechanic, but it turned out someone they knew was: Charlie Taylor—the dude they'd hired to run their bike shop and who had annoyed their sister, Katharine. Though he had little experience repairing motors and never actually built one from scratch, he nonetheless took on the challenge without hesitation.

Charlie once said, "While the boys were handy

with tools, they had never done much machine-work and anyway they were busy on the air-frame. It was up to me." In just six weeks, working in a tiny space above the Wrights' bike shop, Charlie used a sturdy, lightweight aluminum frame to construct a four-cylinder, eight-horsepower gasoline engine that weighed just 152 pounds!

December 14, 1903: Wilbur and the damaged *Flyer* after their unsuccessful first flight attempt.

Once complete, the *Flyer No. 1* was nine feet tall, with a forty-foot wingspan. It boasted two engine-powered propellers and bike wheels for takeoff and landing, and it had a total weight of 605 pounds. That September, the brothers made their way back to Kitty Hawk once again.

It wasn't smooth sailing. On their first test, the engine misfired and had to be fixed. Then one of the propellers cracked and had to be replaced. Next, the bike chain that connected the motor to the propellers snapped. Despite these setbacks, and winter approaching, the brothers kept working.

While they made their final preparations in Kitty Hawk, Samuel Langley and Charles Manly were at it once again in Washington. On December 8, 1903, aboard Langley's houseboat, Manly strapped into the latest *Aerodrome* model. At 4:45 PM, he was catapulted into the air as newspaper reporters and Smithsonian representatives watched. For a very brief moment it seemed as though he would be the first man to fly. A second later the aircraft crumpled, backflipped, and crashed into the icy river.

Manly disappeared beneath the freezing waters with the failed contraption. The crowd of onlookers began to panic when he didn't resurface. Deep below, Manly's flight jacket had become snagged on the wreckage! Charles finally broke free of the sinking plane and surfaced in the nick of time. After being pulled aboard the houseboat and wrapped in a dozen heavy blankets, he slammed down a shot of whiskey before, through chattering teeth, he slung a solid paragraph of curse words at Langley for creating a malfunctioning plane that nearly killed him.

This whole powered human flight thing was definitely not for the fainthearted.

Word of Langley's failure reached Dayton, Ohio, the next day, just as Orville left for Kitty

Hawk with newly fashioned propellers. Two days later he arrived and shared the "good" news with his brother—there was still time to make history.

On December 14, 1903, just a week after Manly's attempted flight, the Wright brothers were once again ready to attempt a launch. They had

On December 17, 1903, Orville Wright was piloting the *Flyer No. 1* as the brothers made history with the first heavier-than-air plane. They stayed aloft for 59 seconds, covering 852 feet.

constructed a runway along a sloped plain and set up their cameras. With the help of John T. Daniels, a young amateur photographer who had come to see the spectacle, they pushed the *Flyer* into place. To decide who would be the first to fly, they flipped a coin. Wilbur won.

The engine roared loudly as it revved up to full power. A group of young boys dove for cover behind a nearby hill, terrified by the sound and uncertain of what was about to happen. With a jolt and the roar of engine and propeller, the *Wright Flyer* began speeding down the runway. However, just as it gained speed, Wilbur accidentally pulled too hard on the rudder, causing the craft to lurch before landing with a thud. Regardless of his mistake, everything else had worked! Human error was the only hindrance.

Three days later, on the morning of Thursday, December 17, after minor repairs, the Wright brothers readied the *Flyer* once again. Wilbur

December 17, 1903: The damaged *Flyer* after its fourth and final flight.

and Orville shook hands one last time for luck. This time Orville climbed aboard the aircraft, dressed in a coat, tie, and cap, his mustache blowing in the wind. Few had turned out in the freezing cold of the North Carolina winter.

Orville started down the runway, with Wilbur running alongside the wing. Then, at approximately 10:35 AM, Orville pulled gently back on the stick, the nose of the aircraft lifted up from the runway, and with a graceful, powerful lift the *Wright Flyer* was airborne! At that moment, photographer John T. Daniels clicked the shutter, capturing one of the most famous photographs in history. Twelve seconds later, the plane sank back to the ground, landing smoothly on its landing gear. They'd done it. On their second attempt, the biplane soared for 59 seconds, covering an incredible 852 feet.

There was no doubt. The Wright brothers had just flown the first powered airplane. Unlike other experimental aircraft at the time, the *Wright Flyer* was able to take off and land under its own power and had unprecedented control over its direction. It was "the first manned, powered, heavier-than-air, and controlled flight." The 1903 *Flyer* would never fly again. Today it sits in the Smithsonian Air and Space Museum, and there's a picture of it on the license plates in North Carolina.

Daniels later said, "It wasn't luck that made

them fly; it was hard work and common sense; they put their whole heart and soul and all their energy into an idea and they had the faith."

Orville immediately telegrammed their father from the weather station, starting with one triumphant word: "SUCCESS."

RECEIVED at   170

176 C KA CS 33 Paid.   Via Norfolk Va

Kitty Hawk N C Dec 17

Bishop M Wright

            7 Hawthorne St

Success four flights thursday morning all against twenty one mile
wind started from Level with engine power alone average speed
through air thirty one miles longest 57 seconds inform Press
home ~~there~~ Christmas .   Orevelle Wright   525P

Orville's telegram to his father proclaiming "success"

CHAPTER 9
It's a Bird, It's a Biplane!
1908

"I recognized at once they were really scientific explorers who were serving the world in much the same way that Columbus had when he discovered America."

—Amos I. Root

Word quickly spread around the world of the Wright brothers' success. While many were amazed, many more were skeptical about whether this whole "airplane" thing would really take off. Was such a thing actually possible? Were the Wright brothers telling the truth? And if they were, would human flight change human history, or was it just a fun hobby for daredevils and stuntmen?

The Wright brothers were ecstatic, but they knew they still had a ton of work to do to make their invention even better. So when the guys returned to Dayton, they went right back to the drawing board and started working on improvements and adjustments. They still ran the bicycle shop, because they needed to keep making money to fund their experiments, but from this point on these guys had one thing in mind, and that was to make an even better airplane.

From the moment the Wrights proved flight was possible, aviation and airplane technology started improving at an incredible rate. You know how video games from six or seven years ago look terrible when compared with the graphics consoles can produce today? It was kind of like that with airplanes in the early 1900s. If the *Wright Flyer* were an old-school Nintendo, the planes being made five years later were like a PlayStation 2.

Because the Wrights no longer had to depend on wind, hills, and weather to make their aircraft work, they didn't need to keep traveling to

By 1905, the Wrights' improved *Flyer* was staying airborne for more than thirty minutes at a time above Huffman Prairie in Dayton.

Kitty Hawk every time they wanted to test one of their designs. They rented a big, open field at a place called Huffman Prairie, which wasn't too far from their home, and continued their mission. People would come from far and wide to watch their remarkable invention, and by 1905 the Wrights were flying a plane called the *Flyer III*, which could do figure eights in the air, stay airborne for thirty-three minutes, and cover nearly twenty miles! Not bad considering their first flight lasted just twelve seconds. The Wrights also had their airplane-control system patented in 1906, meaning they could finally start making money selling their designs.

That same year, Ernest Archdeacon, a wealthy French aviator (and founder of the Aéro-Club de France) called out the Wright brothers and accused them of being a couple of lying frauds. In a letter to the *New York Herald*, he wrote: "The Wrights have flown or they have not flown. They possess a machine or they do not possess one. They are in fact either fliers or liars. It is difficult to fly. It's easy to say, 'We have flown.'"

I don't have to tell you that these are fighting words.

In response, the Wright brothers packed up

their aircraft in 1908 and made their way to France with Katharine to dispel the doubts once and for all. They spent the next year demonstrating their plane in more than two hundred flights across Europe. For a generation that had grown up using horses as the primary mode of transportation, it must have been amazing to watch these siblings soar through the air in a canvas-and-wood glider powered by wooden propellers and a four-cylinder car engine. The Wrights became world-renowned celebrities. They were VIP guests everywhere they went, treated to fancy dinners in the courts of the kings and queens of Europe—and after watching the exhibition in Paris, even Ernest Archdeacon admitted he was wrong.

As the Wright brothers returned home (by boat, because the first plane capable of traveling across the Atlantic Ocean wouldn't be developed for ten more years), they heard that

The Wright brothers, in a horse-drawn carriage, are welcomed home to Dayton by a crowd of fans.

President Howard Taft was arranging a huge parade for them through the streets of New York City. But the Wright brothers didn't really care about that; all they wanted to do was go home to

Dayton and get back to work on their new ideas, so they told the president, "Thanks, but no thanks."

All the same, when Wilbur and Orville arrived in Dayton, tens of thousands of cheering fans greeted them, swarming around the train to welcome them home. The entire city shut down for two days to have a big party celebrating the boys' accomplishments.

CHAPTER 10
The Wright Stuff—
Pioneers of the Sky

1909–Today

"Success is not measured by what a man accomplishes, but by the opposition he has encountered and the courage with which he has maintained the struggle against overwhelming odds."

—Charles Lindbergh

The Wright brothers got back to work designing bigger and better planes. Late in 1908 they approached the army to try to sell the airplane as something it could use in warfare. You couldn't really put guns or bombs on a plane in 1908, but Orville and Wilbur told the generals that the airplane would be a great machine to gather reconnaissance and intelligence on enemy troop positions. It was fast, you could see long distances from up in the sky, and it was pretty hard for a guy standing on the ground to shoot one down.

The army was curious, so it had the Wright brothers come and give a demonstration. Orville took an army officer up in the two-seater *Military Flyer* and flew him around to show him what it was all about. Things were going well, but then, out of nowhere, the controls stopped responding! Orville fought with the control stick, trying to regain some lift, but the *Military Flyer* began spiraling down fast. It plummeted several hundred feet, then smashed *hard* into the dirt, crumpling into wreckage and sending bits of plane scattering in every direction. Orville Wright was seriously injured and needed to go to the hospital. Lieutenant Thomas Selfridge wasn't so lucky . . . He became the first person in history to die in a plane crash.

1908: Bystanders struggle to help Orville Wright and Thomas Selfridge from the wreckage of the world's first fatal plane crash.

Despite almost dying, wrecking his plane, and accidentally killing someone, Orville recovered, worked with Wilbur to rebuild a new *Military Flyer*, and took it back to the army just one year after his wreck. In July 1909 Orville again took the controls, taking Lieutenant Benjamin Foulois up in a new version of the *Flyer*.

This test flight was an unqualified success, and not just because no one died. Wright and Foulois's flight in the *Military Flyer* broke every aviation record in the books—longest flight, fastest top speed, and highest altitude. Racing through the skies at nearly fifty miles an hour, Orville dove, climbed, banked, and turned through the air with ease. The army was so impressed it bought the plane for $30,000—the equivalent of almost a million dollars today!

Benjamin Foulois, the brave soul who sat in the same seat where a fellow soldier had died just a year before, went on to have a pretty interesting life. For the next year and a half he was the only airplane pilot, navigator, instructor, observer, and trainer in the US military—he was literally the entire US Air Force all by himself! Foulois would go on to fly America's first military aviation mission, build a radio that could

Benjamin Foulois: the US military's first trained pilot

communicate between the airplane and the ground, serve in World War I, and eventually retire as the chief of the Army Air Service after thirty-seven years in the military.

1915: Orville and Katharine Wright sitting in the Wright Model HS airplane.

The brothers formed the Wright Company and started selling their airplanes to anyone who could afford them. They sold military planes and civilian planes, and they opened the Wright

Flying School at Huffman Prairie in 1910 to train young pilots.

Amid their success, however, tragedy struck. In 1912 Wilbur Wright contracted typhoid fever—the same disease that had almost killed his brother many years earlier. Wilbur, however, did not overcome the illness, and he died on May 30 at the age of just forty-five.

After Wilbur's death, Orville and Katharine kept his dream alive, traveling the world and selling their biplanes to a generation of new aviation enthusiasts. But running the business wasn't the same without his big brother, and Orville Wright sold the Wright Company in 1915. He used his time and resources to run a printing company, and he also served in President Woodrow Wilson's National Advisory Committee for Aeronautics—the government agency now known as the National Aeronautics and Space Administration: NASA. Back then, they built airplanes, and today they send humans into outer space. Orville also developed a new type of airplane flap, built a couple of seaplanes, and even designed an encryption machine that was used to send coded messages during World War II.

The Wright Company continued to be at the forefront of aviation for the next hundred or so

Charles Lindbergh (second from right) visiting Orville Wright (second from left) at Wright Field in Ohio in June, 1927.

years. It merged with the company of another pioneering aviator, Glenn Hammond Curtiss, in 1929, creating the Curtiss-Wright Corporation. It was the biggest airplane manufacturer in the world, producing thousands of aircraft and engines. In 1921 world-famous aviatrix Amelia Earhart learned to fly on a Curtiss plane. In 1927 Charles Lindbergh became the first man to ever fly solo across the Atlantic Ocean, and he did it with a Wright Company J-5C engine under the hood of his plane. During World War II, the Curtiss P-40 Warhawk was one of the most successful and deadliest fighter planes in the US military, piloted by guys like the Flying Tigers and the Black Sheep Squadron. The Curtiss-Wright Corporation produced fourteen thousand P-40s during the war, plus seven thousand Helldiver torpedo planes, three thousand C-46 transports, and more than 142,000 aircraft engines.

Here's something you might not have realized:

the Curtiss-Wright Corporation still operates to this day. It quit making airplanes after World War II, but it makes key components used in a variety of high-tech vehicles and weapons systems. It builds navigation systems for Air Force drones, weapons stabilizers for the M1 Abrams tank and M2 Bradley fighting vehicle, sensor systems for the F-35 Lightning II jet fighter, and electronics components for Black Hawk, Apache, and Chinook helicopters. It also builds nuclear-propulsion systems for military submarines, aircraft-launch equipment for US aircraft carriers, mechanical actuation systems and flap controls for Boeing, McDonnell Douglas, and Airbus commercial airliners, and even steering and suspension controls for city buses and high-octane race cars. Today the Curtiss-Wright Corporation employs more than ten thousand people and makes billions of dollars. Which isn't bad considering it started a hundred years ago as two brothers building bicycles in their garage.

Orville Wright died in 1948 at the age of seventy-six. The year before he died, he read the news that a daring test pilot named Chuck Yeager had become the first man to travel faster than the speed of sound, when he broke Mach 1 in a Bell X-1 jet airplane. When he'd first built a glider out of canvas and wood in 1900, Orville certainly couldn't have imagined his invention being taken to such an extreme level.

It wasn't always easy, and there was plenty of pain and heartbreak, but today the Wright brothers are among the most famous names in American history. For all the ups and downs of their careers, these men constantly persevered. They never let their failures get the better of them, never let anyone tell them something couldn't be done, and never gave up on their dreams. They started as a couple of high school dropouts, crashing planes on the hot sands of Kitty Hawk, worried about embarrassing themselves in front of their heroes, and today their childhood home is a national museum. Their work hangs in the Smithsonian Institution, and their contributions are so important to the history of aviation that when Neil Armstrong landed Apollo 11 and became the first human to walk on the moon in 1969, he carried with him a piece of the original wing and propeller from the 1903 *Wright Flyer*.

Think about that the next time someone tells you that something "can't be done."

TIMELINE

852   Armen Firman's failed attempt at flight in Córdoba, Spain

1665   Isaac Newton discovers the law of gravity

1783   The Montgolfier brothers create the world's first hot air balloon in France

1867   Wilbur Wright is born in Indiana

1871   Orville Wright is born in Dayton, Ohio

1889   Otto Lilienthal publishes *Bird-Flight as the Basis for Aviation*

1892   Wilbur and Orville get into the bicycle business

1894   Sir Hiram Maxim's steam-powered biplane test fails

1899   The Wright brothers build their first glider in Dayton, Ohio

1900   Von Zeppelin creates the first hydrogen dirigible

1900   The Wright brothers test their first human-piloted glider at Kill Devil Hills in Kitty Hawk, North Carolina

1901   The Wrights have their first major setback with their second glider

1902   The Wright brothers crack the flight equation with their third glider and are able to control the flight along all three axes

1903   Samuel Langley's *Aerodrome* fails both test flights

1903   Orville and Wilbur Wright successfully test the first powered/controlled airplane, becoming the "first in flight" on December 17

1905   The Wright brothers developed the *Flyer III*—a refined version of their airplane

1908   The Wrights demonstrated their airplane in flights across America and Europe

1912   Wilbur Wright dies

1914   World War I begins—airplanes are used in combat for the first time

1927   Charles Lindbergh's transatlantic flight from New York to Paris

1947   Chuck Yeager breaks the sound barrier with the X-1

1948   Orville Wright dies

ACKNOWLEDGMENTS

The authors would like to give thanks to our excellent editor, Simon Boughton, for believing in this project and giving us the opportunity to write it, and to our agent, Farley Chase of Chase Literary, for helping us work out all the details to make this happen.

Erik: I would like to first thank Ben for the amazing opportunity to work on this project—it really is a dream come true. I, of course, want to acknowledge all my friends and family for their support over the years, as well as anyone and everyone who has ever encouraged me to keep on writing.

A very special shout-out to: David Kowalski (for helping to brainstorm the concept of writing about historical failures), Chris Carroll (for introducing me to blogging), Justin Ache (for helping me redesign my website and hosting it), James Lester (for inspiring me to keep the history blog going), Neil Sindicich (for giving me the opportunity to build up my online writing portfolio), Max Michaels (for my first writing gig in print), Damian Fox (for pushing me to pursue publication and helping me put together my first pitch), John Wesley Moody (my college history professor), Jason Whitmarsh (my humanities professor), my Patreon patrons who have financially supported my blogging habit over the years, and to Dani Slader—who put up with me every step of the way.

Finally, I want to thank Meg—for her endless support and love during the craziest year of my life.

(If I missed anyone, it's only because I'm already way over my word count.)

Ben: I would like to thank Connie Hsu of Three Rivers for putting my name in to work on this project and finally giving us the opportunity to work together again (even if it is in a rather tangential fashion). I'd also like to thank my family and friends, who have always been there for me throughout all the crazy ups and downs I've had these past few years: Mom, Dad, Clay, John, Barbara, Scarlett, Matt, Brian, and all my D&D crew. Thank you also to my wonderful intern and research assistant, Alyssa Isaacks, for her help proofreading and fact-checking the final manuscript and to the lovely and amazing Thais Melo, who is by far my favorite engineer.

BIBLIOGRAPHY

Aviation History Online Museum: aviation-history.com.

Bonds, Ray, ed. *The Story of Aviation: A Concise History of Flight*. London: Greenhill Books, 1997.

Britten, Loretta, and Paul Mathless. *Our American Century: Century of Flight*. Alexandria, VA: Time-Life Books, 1999.

Crompton, Samuel Willard. *The Wright Brothers: First in Flight*. New York: Chelsea House, 2007.

Curtiss-Wright Corporation: curtisswright.com.

Dixon-Engel, Tara, and Mike Jackson. *The Wright Brothers: First in Flight*. New York: Sterling, 2007.

Goldstone, Lawrence. *Birdmen: The Wright Brothers, Glenn Curtiss, and the Battle to Control the Skies*. New York: Ballantine Books, 2014.

Gunston, Bill. *Aviation: Year by Year*. New York: DK, 2001.

Heppenheimer, T. A. *A Brief History of Flight: From Balloons to Mach 3 and Beyond*. New York: Wiley, 2001.

Jeffrey, Gary. *The History of Flight*. New York: Rosen, 2008.

Kelly, Fred C. *The Wright Brothers*. New York: Dover, 2009.

McCullough, David. *The Wright Brothers*. New York: Simon & Schuster, 2015.

National Aviation Hall of Fame: nationalaviation.org.

Niccoli, Riccardo. *History of Flight: From the Flying Machine of Leonardo da Vinci to the Conquest of Space*. Vercelli, Italy: White Star, 2006.

Old, Wendie C., and Robert Andrew Parker. *To Fly: The Story of the Wright Brothers*. New York: Clarion, 2002.

Rausch, Monica L. *The Wright Brothers and the Airplane.* Milwaukee, WI: Weekly Reader, 2007.

Taylor, Michael J. H. *Aviators: A Photographic History of Flight.* New York: HarperCollins, 2005.

Tobin, James. *To Conquer the Air: The Wright Brothers and the Great Race to Flight.* New York: Free Press, 2003.

Welch, Becky. *The Wright Brothers: Conquering the Sky.* New York: Ballantine Books, 1992.

Wright Brothers Aeroplane Company Virtual Museum of Pioneer Aviation: wright-brothers.org.

PICTURE CREDITS

Page 14–15: Wikimedia Commons; **16–17:** Wikimedia Commons; **30:** Library of Congress Prints and Photographs Division, LC-DIG-ppmsca-08396; **30:** Library of Congress Prints and Photographs Division, Wright Brothers Negatives, LC-DIG-ppprs-00676; **35:** Library of Congress Prints and Photographs Division, LC-DIG-ppmsca-02545; **44:** Manuscript Division, Library of Congress; **54:** Library of Congress Prints and Photographs Division, Wright Brothers Negatives, LC-DIG-ppprs-00545; **55:** Library of Congress Prints and Photographs Division, Wright Brothers Negatives, LC-DIG-ppprs-00556; **56:** Library of Congress Prints and Photographs Division, Wright Brothers Negatives, LC-DIG-ppprs-00544; **66:** Library of Congress Prints and Photographs Division, Wright Brothers Negatives, LC-DIG-ppprs-00570; **73:** Library of Congress Prints and Photographs Division, Wright Brothers Negatives, LC-DIG-ppprs-00603; **78:** Wikimedia Commons; **81:** Library of Congress Prints and Photographs Division, Wright Brothers Negatives, LC-DIG-ppprs-00610; **84:** Library of Congress Prints and Photographs Division, Wright Brothers Negatives, LC-DIG-ppprs-00626; **86:** Library of Congress Prints and Photographs Division, Wright Brothers Negatives, LC-DIG-ppprs-00614; **88:** Prints and Photographs Division, Library of Congress; **91:** Library of Congress Prints and Photographs Division, Wright Brothers Negatives, LC-DIG-ppprs-00658; **95:** Courtesy of Special Collections & Archives, Wright State University; **99:** Wreck of the Wright Brothers Flyer; 9/17/1908; Records of the Department of Defense. **101:** Library of Congress Prints and Photographs Division, Bain Collection, LC-DIG-ggbain-05926; **102:** Library of Congress Prints and Photographs Division, Wright Brothers Negatives, LC-DIG-ppprs-00588; **104:** Library of Congress Prints and Photographs Division, Wright Brothers Negatives, LC-DIG-ppprs-00694.

INDEX

Numbers in **bold** indicate pages with illustrations